For Such a One as I

Patricia Ramsden

Parson's Porch Books

www.parsonsporchbooks.com

For Such a One as I

ISBN: Softcover 1-978-1-949888-98-0

Copyright © 2019 by Patricia Ramsden

All rights reserved. No part of this book may be reproduced or transmitted in any form or by any means, electronic or mechanical, including photocopying, recording, or by any information storage and retrieval system, without permission in writing from the publisher.

Scripture quotations taken from The Holy Bible, New International Version® NIV® Copyright © 1973 1978 1984 2011 by Biblica, Inc. TM Used by permission. All rights reserved worldwide.

For Such a One as I

Contents

Preface 7

Palm Sunday
It Is Time 9
Fetch Me A Colt 11
Not Everyone Loves A Parade 13
At The End Of Triumph 14
By A Strength Not His Own 15

The Passing Days
For Those With Ears To Hear 19
The Rabbi 20
A Holy Unholy Week 21
Good Intentions 22
Foolish or Wise? 24
What Is Heaven Worth? 25
Remembering 26
An Anointing 28
Hypocrites 29
Not A Stone Upon Stone 30
Render Unto God 31
The End Is Coming 32
Judgment Day 33
A Withered Believer 35
What Will You Give Me? 38
Be On Guard 39
Before Christ/After Christ 40
Priests Plotting 41

Maundy Thursday
It Was Time 45
Bread, Wine 46
Before The Rooster Crows 47
Mystery Divine 48

In The Garden of Gethsemane

The Garden 51
Sans 52
Fleeing Into Darkness 53
In That Upper Room 54
Betrayal 55

Before the Dawn of Friday's Morn

Not A Word 59
Who Wields The Whip? 60
Stripped Bare 62
Pilate 63

Good Friday

Isn't This The Passover? 69
A Woman 70
Friday's Parade 71
Mary, Mother of Jesus 72
I Am The One 73
The Tree of Life 75

Holy Saturday

The Battle Continues 79
He Descended Into Hell 80

Easter Sunday

Easter Born 83
Easter's Symphony 84
What If... 85
Sing Us Into Light 86
Everything Became Clear 87
The Road Home 88
Thomas 89

Preface

I wrote these poems by a running stream in the Great Smoky Mountains with beauty all around and a heaviness in my heart. I wrote them on long walks through familiar byways. I wrote them morning, noon, and deep within the night. They are reflections on how the various participants of Holy Week might have felt during their part of the saga and of how I reflected upon the incidents of the week in my own life as well. While the high holy days are an integral part of the text, much attention is given to the teachings of Jesus during the days of Holy Week. May this book be the same source of unease for you as it has been for me as we each make our own journey through these most holy days.

Yours in Christ,
Patricia Ramsden

Mark 11:1-2

As they approached Jerusalem and came to Bethphage and Bethany at the Mount of Olives, Jesus sent two of his disciples, **2** *saying to them, "Go to the village ahead of you, and just as you enter it, you will find a colt tied there, which no one has ever ridden. Untie it and bring it here.*

It is Time

It is time.
Go.
Fetch the ass for me to ride.
I must enter David's holy city.

It is time
For the gauntlet of temptations
As Satan shows me what could be
If I would only bend
If I would only break.

It is time
For we both know of the parade
Yet to come.
Shouts of Hosanna
Will all too soon
Become cries of crucify.
All this as Satan whispers
It is time.

I have the power
To make earthly dreams come true.
It would be such an easy thing to do.
But I am bound
To the reality of eternity's prayer
And it is time.

Once again I whisper
Into the shouts of praise
"Get thee behind me Satan."

It is time.
Let the parade of temptations begin.

Zechariah 9:9
Rejoice greatly, Daughter Zion! Shout, Daughter Jerusalem! See, your king comes to you, righteous and victorious, lowly and riding on a donkey, on a colt, the foal of a donkey.

Fetch Me A Colt

Go. Fetch me a colt —
A humble beast bearing its burden
Without complaint.
For I come in heavenly peace
Not to render judgement without mercy
But with the gift of undeserved grace.

Mark 11: 7- 10

7 When they brought the colt to Jesus and threw their cloaks over it, he sat on it. 8 Many people spread their cloaks on the road, while others spread branches they had cut in the fields. 9 Those who went ahead and those who followed shouted, "Hosanna!" "Blessed is he who comes in the name of the Lord! 10 Blessed is the coming kingdom of our father David! Hosanna in the highest heaven!"

A Celebrity Parade

Throw down your branches!
Raise up your hands!
Shout your Hosannas!
Our long years of waiting have ended!
The Messiah has come!

Roll out the red carpet!
Demand His autograph!
Rush His long, low limousine!

Take Him by force!
Hoist Him on your shoulders!
Our Savior has arrived!
Prosperity is ours!
We shall be blessed!

Hosanna!
Our king has come!

John 12: 13-16, 19

__13__ They took palm branches and went out to meet him, shouting, "Hosanna!" "Blessed is he who comes in the name of the Lord!" "Blessed is the king of Israel!" __14__ Jesus found a young donkey and sat on it, as it is written:

__15__ "Do not be afraid, Daughter Zion; see, your king is coming, seated on a donkey's colt." __16__ At first his disciples did not understand all this. Only after Jesus was glorified did they realize that these things had been written about him and that these things had been done to him. __19__ So the Pharisees said to one another, "See, this is getting us nowhere. Look how the whole world has gone after him!"

Not Everyone Loves A Parade

Sorrow.
Pain.
Reality in all its madness
Mingle with shouts of praise.
A Messiah has at long last arrived
Holding the promises of the ages.

Abundant life.
Healing.
Riches beyond imagining.
Freedom from Rome.
Dreams
Hopes
Bind this man
As surely as in a prisoner's chains.

Matthew 21: 8-9

8 A very large crowd spread their cloaks on the road, while others cut branches from the trees and spread them on the road. 9 The crowds that went ahead of him and those that followed shouted, "Hosanna to the Son of David!" "Blessed is he who comes in the name of the Lord!" "Hosanna in the highest heaven!"

At the End of Triumph

Text comes alive.
Prophecy co-mingles with reality.
No wonder they shouted.

Yet He knew
Cheers would so quickly
Turn to jeers and
Shouts of "Hosanna" into cries of "crucify."
For at the end of their dreams of triumph
Waited a whip and a cross.

Matthew 21: 12-13

12 Jesus entered the temple courts and drove out all who were buying and selling there. He overturned the tables of the money changers and the benches of those selling doves. 13 "It is written," he said to them, "'My house will be called a house of prayer,' but you are making it 'a den of robbers.'"

By A Strength Not His Own

Clutching the whip
Teeth clinched.
Eyes weeping.
By a strength not his own, He raged.
With a grief unleashed,
He cleansed the temple.

The Passing Days

Luke 21: 37-38

37 Each day Jesus was teaching at the temple, and each evening he went out to spend the night on the hill called the Mount of Olives, 38 and all the people came early in the morning to hear him at the temple.

For Those with Ears to Hear

He came in each morning,
Out by evening's fall
Teaching hard words
To even harder hearts.

He came in each morning,
Out by evening's fall
For those with ears to hear
And hearts to listen.

He comes in each morning....

Matthew 21: 23

23 Jesus entered the temple courts, and, while he was teaching, the chief priests and the elders of the people came to him. "By what authority are you doing these things?" they asked. "And who gave you this authority?"

The Rabbi

The rabbi sat on temple steps
In his roughhewn robe
Worn from traveling.
Hands on His knees
Day after day
Teaching.
Explaining.
Telling stories.
He teaches us
Under his own authority.
He needs no other.

Mark 11:18
18 The chief priests and the teachers of the law heard this and began looking for a way to kill him, for they feared him, because the whole crowd was amazed at his teaching.

Matthew 22:22
22 When they heard this, they were amazed. So they left him and went away.

A Holy Unholy Week

Sadducees
Pharisees
Pilgrims
All
Stand silently,
Arms crossed.
Some disapproving.
Some listening.
Some nodding in agreement.
Some touched by love.
All waiting
They knew not for what.
Amazed at His teaching
They feared Him.

Matthew 21: 28-31

28 "What do you think? There was a man who had two sons. He went to the first and said, 'Son, go and work today in the vineyard.' 29 "'I will not,' he answered, but later he changed his mind and went. 30 "Then the father went to the other son and said the same thing. He answered, 'I will, sir,' but he did not go. 31 "Which of the two did what his father wanted?" "The first," they answered. Jesus said to them, "Truly I tell you; the tax collectors and the prostitutes are entering the kingdom of God ahead of you."

Good Intentions

I had the best of intentions.
Really I did.
I was going to go visit him
There on his unit
Where memories were vanquished.
Truly I was going to go.
But…
My house needed cleaning.
What was I to do?
I know he'll understand.

I had the best of intentions.
Really I did.
I wanted to see Mom
To ooh and ahh and lie
About the small apartment
Away from familiar faces and places
But …
My friends asked me out
So I had lunch instead.
I know she'll understand.

I had the best of intentions.
Really I did.
But there was a text I needed to take
More than that sweet hour of prayer
Surely God will understand.

I had the best of intentions....

Matthew 25: 1 - 10

"At that time the kingdom of heaven will be like ten virgins who took their lamps and went out to meet the bridegroom. 2 Five of them were foolish and five were wise. 3 The foolish ones took their lamps but did not take any oil with them. 4 The wise ones, however, took oil in jars along with their lamps. 5 The bridegroom was a long time in coming, and they all became drowsy and fell asleep.

6 "At midnight the cry rang out: 'Here's the bridegroom! Come out to meet him!'

7 "Then all the virgins woke up and trimmed their lamps. 8 The foolish ones said to the wise,

'Give us some of your oil; our lamps are going out.'

9 "'No,' they replied, 'there may not be enough for both us and you. Instead, go to those who sell oil and buy some for yourselves.'

10 "But while they were on their way to buy the oil, the bridegroom arrived. The virgins who were ready went in with him to the wedding banquet. And the door was shut.

Foolish or Wise?

I have lost you in the darkness of midnight.
Now I long once more for light.
Please.
I'm begging.
Give me the oil of your presence once more.

Luke 21: 1-4

As Jesus looked up, he saw the rich putting their gifts into the temple treasury. 2 He also saw a poor widow put in two very small copper coins. 3 "Truly I tell you," he said, "this poor widow has put in more than all the others. 4 All these people gave their gifts out of their wealth; but she out of her poverty put in all she had to live on."

What Is Heaven Worth?

A woman weighed down in weariness
Puts a single hard-earned dollar
In the offering plate.

A man puts in a check
Not even close to a tithe
Yet wealth indeed.
He stares at the lone dollar
And shakes his head.
What can a mere dollar be worth
In the eyes of God?

Everything.
It is worth everything
To the kingdom of God.

Luke 2: 42-47

42 When he was twelve years old, they went up to the festival, according to the custom. 43 After the festival was over, while his parents were returning home, the boy Jesus stayed behind in Jerusalem, but they were unaware of it. 44 Thinking he was in their company, they traveled on for a day. Then they began looking for him among their relatives and friends. 45 When they did not find him, they went back to Jerusalem to look for him. 46 After three days they found him in the temple courts, sitting among the teachers, listening to them and asking them questions. 47 Everyone who heard him was amazed at his understanding and his answers.

Remembering

He sat on the temple steps
Alone
Remembering
Past
Present
Future
They meld into one.

He was twelve at the time
There in that Jerusalem past
Sitting on those same steps
Talking with the teachers
Men of the Law.
They were moments of purest joy.
Arguing.
Debating.
Sharing visions.

Then His frantic parents came
And He was dragged away
From the true home of His Abba

To their home in Nazareth.

He sat
Quiet in the past
Alone
Waiting to be dragged away once more
From this, his true home.

Mark 14: 3-9

3 While he was in Bethany, reclining at the table in the home of Simon the Leper, a woman came with an alabaster jar of very expensive perfume, made of pure nard. She broke the jar and poured the perfume on his head. 4 Some of those present were saying indignantly to one another, "Why this waste of perfume? 5 It could have been sold for more than a year's wages and the money given to the poor." And they rebuked her harshly.

6 "Leave her alone," said Jesus. "Why are you bothering her? She has done a beautiful thing to me. 7 The poor you will always have with you, and you can help them any time you want. But you will not always have me. 8 She did what she could. She poured perfume on my body beforehand to prepare for my burial. 9 Truly I tell you, wherever the gospel is preached throughout the world, what she has done will also be told, in memory of her."

An Anointing

Slowly I took down my hair
Letting it fall like rain
In the midst of a storm.
My tears washed
His tired, road worn feet.
I poured out
My fears
My doubts
My hopes
My dreams
My precious oil
In fearful anticipation
Of what was to come.

Matthew 23: 29-33

29 "Woe to you, teachers of the law and Pharisees, you hypocrites! You build tombs for the prophets and decorate the graves of the righteous. 30 And you say, 'If we had lived in the days of our ancestors, we would not have taken part with them in shedding the blood of the prophets.' 31 So you testify against yourselves that you are the descendants of those who murdered the prophets. 32 Go ahead, then, and complete what your ancestors started! 33 "You snakes! You brood of vipers! How will you escape being condemned to hell?

Hypocrites

Hypocrites dress in priestly robes
Throughout the ages
Shouting their "thou shalt nots"
In condemning voices.
Justifying their own sins
Contorting the scriptures
Building their own glory
In ornate temples and
Mansions not over the hillside.

"Woe to you, you hypocrites…
How will you escape
Being condemned to hell?"

Luke 21: 5-6

5 Some of his disciples were remarking about how the temple was adorned with beautiful stones and with gifts dedicated to God. But Jesus said, 6 "As for what you see here, the time will come when not one stone will be left on another; every one of them will be thrown down."

Not A Stone Upon Stone

Like the widow
Putting in her all
Do not put your trust
In money
In buildings
In things of this world.
These and all things shall disappear.
Stone upon stone
Kingdom upon Kingdom
Thing upon thing
Will be torn from you
Till all that is left is
Faith in the Lord

Luke 20: 20-25

20 Keeping a close watch on him, they sent spies, who pretended to be sincere. They hoped to catch Jesus in something he said, so that they might hand him over to the power and authority of the governor. 21 So the spies questioned him: "Teacher, we know that you speak and teach what is right, and that you do not show partiality but teach the way of God in accordance with the truth. 22 Is it right for us to pay taxes to Caesar or not?"

23 He saw through their duplicity and said to them, 24 "Show me a denarius. Whose image and inscription are on it?" "Caesar's," they replied. 25 He said to them, "Then give back to Caesar what is Caesar's, and to God what is God's."

Render unto God

Render unto God?
Ah, but what is God's?

My love.
My life.
My all.

Luke 21:7-11

7 "Teacher," they asked, "when will these things happen? And what will be the sign that they are about to take place?"
8 He replied: "Watch out that you are not deceived. For many will come in my name, claiming, 'I am he,' and, 'The time is near.' Do not follow them. 9 When you hear of wars and uprisings, do not be frightened. These things must happen first, but the end will not come right away."
10 Then he said to them: "Nation will rise against nation, and kingdom against kingdom." 11 There will be great earthquakes, famines and pestilences in various places, and fearful events and great signs from heaven.

The End Is Coming

It was the war to end all wars.
Yet despite all our imaginings
Of everlasting peace,
It wasn't.

Even as men and women lay their weapons down,
The next war lurked in their hearts
And the next and the next and the next
Until all the earth will be consumed by
Violence
Hatred
Jealousy
Fear.

It is then
As always
He shall come.

Matthew 25:37-40

37 "Then the righteous will answer him, 'Lord, when did we see you hungry and feed you, or thirsty and give you something to drink? 38 When did we see you a stranger and invite you in, or needing clothes and clothe you? 39 When did we see you sick or in prison and go to visit you?' 40 "The King will reply, 'Truly I tell you, whatever you did for one of the least of these brothers and sisters of mine, you did for me.'

Judgment Day

You want to know
Of the judgment day
And about how you will be known
As one of mine?

Then hear:

It is not by words alone
Nor songs of praise
Nor fervent prayers.

It is through decisions made.
Actions taken.
Love given.

Feed the hungry
With the bread you bake
Then break the bread of grace
As one with them.

Give to the thirsty
Water turned into fine wine
Sharing the cup of my living love.

Invite the stranger
Into your land, your home, your conscience.
Make of them your brothers and sisters
A family of the heart.

Clothe the naked.
Turn their rags into
Rich robes of joy.

Heal the sick of body and soul
For such is the balm of heaven.

Visit those whose arms
Stretch beyond the cages
You have built for them.
Break the bars of society.
Touch their raw pain.

Do these things and you will see
Not only the welcoming gates of heaven
But the walls surrounding both temple and Eden
Thrown down.

Matthew 21: 18-20

18 Early in the morning, as Jesus was on his way back to the city, he was hungry. 19 Seeing a fig tree by the road, he went up to it but found nothing on it except leaves. Then he said to it, "May you never bear fruit again!" Immediately the tree withered. 20 When the disciples saw this, they were amazed. "How did the fig tree wither so quickly?" they asked.

A Withered Believer

I struggle and hide
From the truth hidden in His words.
How can this be?
I know the meanings others have found
But me?
How often have I become the withered tree
Even in the full bloom of His presence?
I do not want to know.
Truth hurts too much.

Luke 20: 9-16

9 He went on to tell the people this parable: "A man planted a vineyard, rented it to some farmers and went away for a long time. 10 At harvest time he sent a servant to the tenants so they would give him some of the fruit of the vineyard. But the tenants beat him and sent him away empty-handed. 11 He sent another servant, but that one also they beat and treated shamefully and sent away empty-handed. 12 He sent still a third, and they wounded him and threw him out. 13 "Then the owner of the vineyard said, 'What shall I do? I will send my son, whom I love; perhaps they will respect him.' 14 "But when the tenants saw him, they talked the matter over. 'This is the heir,' they said. 'Let's kill him, and the inheritance will be ours.' 15 So they threw him out of the vineyard and killed him. "What then will the owner of the vineyard do to them? 16 He will come and kill those tenants and give the vineyard to others. "When the people heard this, they said, "God forbid!".

Our Landlord

Our landlord thinks
All power is his.
He demands the fruit of our harvest
The labor of our hands.

Yet he has been gone so long
And he is so very far away,
We barely remember him now.

What he said
To our fathers' fathers:
How to give
How to live
Has faded into the yesteryears
Till only faint remembrances remain.

We sent his servants away
Empty-handed
Heavy hearted
Bruised and beaten
Without the fruit of the harvest
So justly demanded.

In desperation
He sent his Son
His only Son
Whom he loved.

Persuaded we would listen
Would at long last heed words
Spoken so long ago
So carefully inscribed upon our hearts.

Instead we threw Love out
Killing him in our greed.

He spoke the parable
Sitting on the temple steps.
Still the question hangs in all eternity,
What will we do to His Son?
His only Son
Whom He loves?

Matthew 26: 14-16
14 Then one of the Twelve—the one called Judas Iscariot—went to the chief priests 15 and asked, "What are you willing to give me if I deliver him over to you?" So they counted out for him thirty pieces of silver. 16 From then on Judas watched for an opportunity to hand him over.

What Will You Give Me?

They answered the unspoken question
Hanging between them in the night.
What will you give me?

What will you give me
To betray my friend?
My teacher?
My Lord?

The question hangs through eternity
Like a man hanging on a cross.

Silver.
Thirty pieces of silver.
Fame.
Riches.
Power beyond compare
If you will only
Betray your Lord.

Done.

Mark 13: 14-16

14 "When you see 'the abomination that causes desolation' standing where it does not belong— let the reader understand—then let those who are in Judea flee to the mountains. 15 Let no one on the housetop go down or enter the house to take anything out. 16 Let no one in the field go back to get their cloak."

Be on Guard

The crystal cathedral
Lies shattered on the ground.
Only sharp shards left
Of a prosperity gospel
Where the rich are blessed
And the poor —

Are not.

When will the horrors come?

Ah, my child, they have already begun.

Luke 21: 25-27

25 "There will be signs in the sun, moon and stars. On the earth, nations will be in anguish and perplexity at the roaring and tossing of the sea. 26 People will faint from terror, apprehensive of what is coming on the world, for the heavenly bodies will be shaken. 27 At that time they will see the Son of Man coming in a cloud with power and great glory."

Before Christ/After Christ

The end is coming!
And so it did.
In ways we could never imagine
The world came to a
Soul searching end
Only to begin again.

Before Christ. After Christ.

Before grace. After grace.

Before love. After love.

Each believer has their own moment of
earth shattering recognition.
Lives interrupted.
Earth quaking moments.
Forever changes
Made time and time again.

One world ends.
A new world begins.

Luke 19:47
Every day he was teaching at the temple. But the chief priests, the teachers of the law and the leaders among the people were trying to kill him.

Priests Plotting

Priests plotting
A believer longing
A stranger passing by.

All listening
All believing
Each in their own way.

Life or death.
These were the final days.

Maundy Thursday

Matthew 26:17-19

17 On the first day of the Festival of Unleavened Bread, the disciples came to Jesus and asked, "Where do you want us to make preparations for you to eat the Passover?" 18 He replied, "Go into the city to a certain man and tell him, 'The Teacher says: My appointed time is near. I am going to celebrate the Passover with my disciples at your house.'" 19 So the disciples did as Jesus had directed them and prepared the Passover.

It Was Time

It was time to prepare.
Time to gather the lamb, wine, and unleavened bread
Time to celebrate freedom from slavery to all masters.
Time to unite past and present.

It was time to prepare.
Time to meet in secret.
Time to bring Herod on board.
Time to arrange for soldiers in the night.
Time to bribe a disciple and a friend.

It was time to prepare.
Time to tell the Story.
Time to remember the journey from slavery to freedom.
Time to join the battle between darkness and light.

It was time to prepare the very lamb of God.

Luke 22:14-20

14 When the hour came, Jesus and his apostles reclined at the table. 15 And he said to them, "I have eagerly desired to eat this Passover with you before I suffer. 16 For I tell you, I will not eat it again until it finds fulfillment in the kingdom of God." 17 After taking the cup, he gave thanks and said, "Take this and divide it among you. 18 For I tell you I will not drink again from the fruit of the vine until the kingdom of God comes." 19 And he took bread, gave thanks and broke it, and gave it to them, saying, "This is my body given for you; do this in remembrance of me." 20 In the same way, after the supper he took the cup, saying, "This cup is the new covenant in my blood, which is poured out for you."

Bread, Wine

Friendship
Laughter
The telling of one story
The making of another
Freedom's journey
Begun with death
Ending in life
A nation born
A people redeemed
Slavery ends
With the promised land

Matthew 26:33-34

33 Peter replied, "Even if all fall away on account of you, I never will."
34 "Truly I tell you," Jesus answered, "this very night, before the rooster crows, you will disown me three times."

Before the Rooster Crows

Even if all fall away,
I will stay.
I'll be
Brave
Courageous
A rescuer
In the night.

Yet in the stillness You knew
In that night of terror I would betray you.

Mark 14: 22-24

22 While they were eating, Jesus took bread, and when he had given thanks, he broke it and gave it to his disciples, saying, "Take it; this is my body." 23 Then he took a cup, and when he had given thanks, he gave it to them, and they all drank from it. 24 "This is my blood of the covenant, which is poured out for many," he said to them.

Mystery Divine

Bread.
Wine.
Mystery divine.

My body.
My blood.

Out of my death
Your life.

Eat your fill.
Consume my grace.
Drink the cup.
Guzzle my love.

Bread.
Wine.
Mystery divine.

In the Garden of Gethsemane

Luke 22: 42-44

42 "Father, if you are willing, take this cup from me; yet not my will, but yours be done." 43 An angel from heaven appeared to him and strengthened him. 44 And being in anguish, he prayed more earnestly, and his sweat was like drops of blood falling to the ground.

The Garden

The Son begs His Father
"Surely there is another way?
Can't you make another way? Please?"

Tears fell as blood.

In desperation He pleads again
"Let this cup pass."
The Father weeps.
Alone
In the grief of No
He carries out eternity's plan.

Mark 14:
50 Then everyone deserted him and fled.

Sans

Running.
Fleeing.
Gasping.
They race
Into darkness
Leaving Him to die alone.
Sans disciples.
Sans companions.
Sans friends.

Matthew 26: 56b
Then all the disciples deserted him and fled.

Fleeing into Darkness

Fleeing into darkness
Breaking promises
As they stumble through the night
I will never betray you.
      I will never desert you.
            I will never…

Mark 14:50

50 Then everyone deserted him and fled.

In That Upper Room

There in that upper room
Signs of the feast
Still strewn around
Silently they hunched down
Into grief and fear
Hurling accusations
Hard words of fatal judgement.

Trembling at each noise
Each foot fall on the stairs
Climbing toward them.

My God.
My God.
How could we desert Him?

In His absence
All He taught,
Each Word He'd said
Haunted them
As they gathered
Once more in that upper room.

Still the whip came down
Stripping flesh from bone
Throughout this
Eternally endless night
Darkness extinguishing Light.

Mark 14: 66-72

66 While Peter was below in the courtyard, one of the servant girls of the high priest came by. 67 When she saw Peter warming himself, she looked closely at him. "You also were with that Nazarene, Jesus," she said.
68 But he denied it. "I don't know or understand what you're talking about," he said, and went out into the entryway. 69 When the servant girl saw him there, she said again to those standing around, "This fellow is one of them." 70 Again he denied it.
After a little while, those standing near said to Peter, "Surely you are one of them, for you are a Galilean." 71 He began to call down curses, and he swore to them, "I don't know this man you're talking about."
72 Immediately the rooster crowed the second time. Then Peter remembered the word Jesus had spoken to him: "Before the rooster crows twice you will disown me three times." And he broke down and wept.

Betrayal

I betrayed Him.
Not with a single word
But word after word
Denying I knew Him.
Denying I followed Him.
Denying I loved Him.

Where shall I find Him now?
When shall I find Him again?

Even here?
Even now?

My Savior
Redeemer
Friend

Before the Dawn of Friday's Morn

Mark 14: 60-62

60 Then the high priest stood up before them and asked Jesus, "Are you not going to answer? What is this testimony that these men are bringing against you?" 61 But Jesus remained silent and gave no answer. Again the high priest asked him, "Are you the Messiah, the Son of the Blessed One?" 62 "I am," said Jesus. "And you will see the Son of Man sitting at the right hand of the Mighty One and coming on the clouds of heaven."

Not A Word

Not a word
In a night filled with words.
Words that betrayed.
Words that judged.
Words that condemned.

Till finally the question
He had come to answer.

"Are you the Christ?"

"I am."

All of heaven sang....
Then wept.

Matthew 27: 26b
But he [Pilate] had Jesus flogged, and handed him over to be crucified.

Who Wields the Whip?

I am not a man.
Not human at all.
In these moments of torture
I left my being long ago
As I stepped
Whip in hand
Into the arena of hell.

Again.
Again.
Again.
And yet again.
My whip tears through
Mangled flesh
Reddened with strands of muscle and blood.
Bones peering out at me barely visible
Through the torture of suffering and pain

Who is this man?
Why does he refuse to scream?
Grant me some pleasure
as I flail you
Again.
Again.
And yet again.

It gives me no satisfaction
Of a job well done
Without the cries for mercy
The desperate futility of
Stop.

The silence of the man
Touches my spirit vanquished by
Uncried howling pain.

There is a fleeting moment.
A remembrance of the long ago.
The memory of a boy playing in fields of joy
Now flogging into a mass of flesh
Man after man
With the stench of death.

Stop.

I am no man.
I have no pity.
Living with demons
Howling
Howling
Like screaming wind
Through what little is left of my soul.

I hear the frantic roars:
Don't kill him.
Not yet.
We have our plans.
There's more to come.

Scream damn you.
Scream into the despairing silence
So my screaming will finally end.

Mark 15: 6-14

6 Now it was the custom at the festival to release a prisoner whom the people requested. 7 A man called Barabbas was in prison with the insurrectionists who had committed murder in the uprising. 8 The crowd came up and asked Pilate to do for them what he usually did. 9 "Do you want me to release to you the king of the Jews?" asked Pilate, 10 knowing it was out of self-interest that the chief priests had handed Jesus over to him. 11 But the chief priests stirred up the crowd to have Pilate release Barabbas instead. 12 "What shall I do, then, with the one you call the king of the Jews?" Pilate asked them. 13 "Crucify him!" they shouted. 14 "Why? What crime has he committed?" asked Pilate. But they shouted all the louder, "Crucify him!"

Stripped Bare

Bones stripped of flesh
By nail studded whips
A crown of thorns piercing his head
The sounds of the crowd
Through the haze of pain
Crying "Crucify!"

They too easily betrayed Him
with their frenzied shouts
"Give us Barabbas!"

They knew —
We knew —
In those sacred moments
What kind of Savior He was.
He is.

We did not care.

Matthew 27: 24

24 When Pilate saw that he was getting nowhere, but that instead an uproar was starting, he took water and washed his hands in front of the crowd. "I am innocent of this man's blood," he said. "It is your responsibility!"

Pilate

Who is this man
That they want so much to
Kill him?

I had him scourged.
Surely that should be enough.

But no.

I had him whipped.
So they whipped the crowd
Into a turmoil of emotion.

"Look at them" they said
"They will riot on our command".

I knew they were right.

I must keep the peace
At all costs
I must keep the peace
Who is this man?
These warring priests long to sacrifice
On the altar of their power.

More flogging.
More agony.
Guards brought him to me
Once more
This bloody mass of flesh pooling red
On my white marbled floors.

Who is this man
Lifting his eyes in compassion
For me?
Fall to your knees!
Beg for compassion
From me
Not for me!

Who is this man
Who fancies himself a king
Sent from heavenly places
Descended to earth
To dwell in hell
Before me?

Still they shout "Crucify".

I wash my hands of him.
Let them pronounce his fate.
I am cleansing myself of this
Entire
Bloody
Affair.

Yet the question lingers:
Who is this man?

Heaven and earth
Wait with baited breath
Through the centuries

Who do **you** say that I am?
His — our — answer echoes.

Crucify him.

Good Friday

Luke 23: 27

27 A large number of people followed him, including women who mourned and wailed for him.

Isn't This the Passover?

She pushed through the holiday crowd
As they bought up their souvenirs.

Did they not see
Did they not hear
The wrenching moans
As they whipped out this man's life
Heavy burdened by a cross?

Faithful women
Weeping
As they follow behind
This God
Forsaken
Man
Stumbling
Bleeding
Through God's holy city
In this holy time.

After all,
Isn't this the Passover?
The pass over of God?

Luke 23: 27

27 A large number of people followed him, including women who mourned and wailed for him.

A Woman

I tore at my cloths
And wiped His face of agony

"Who are you?"
The words could barely be heard above
The pain of eternity.

I am woman
Weeping
Wailing
Woman
Throughout the ages
In desperation
Wiping away at the pain of the world.

Luke 23: 26

26 As the soldiers led him away, they seized Simon from Cyrene, who was on his way in from the country, and put the cross on him and made him carry it behind Jesus.

Friday's Parade

I pushed and pulled my way
Through the crowd
Toward this man —
This bleeding, wretch of a man —
Whipped forward like a tortured mongrel
A joke of a man.

Scorned
Laughed at
Spat upon.

I stumbled onto rough hewn stones
Lunging to relieve His pain
Forced to bear His cross

We
Together
Climbed the hill
To Calvary.

John 19: 25

25 Near the cross of Jesus stood his mother, his mother's sister, Mary the wife of Clopas, and Mary Magdalene.

Mary, Mother of Jesus

I wept tears of joy
The moment You were born
I held You in my arms
Nuzzled You at my breast.
I watched as You grew –
A small boy wading in the water.
A teen learning a carpenter's trade.
A young man grown too soon
Caring for our family.

You were the One who held me,
Comforted me,
When Joseph died.
It was You that I released
To the mission You were born for –
A mission of love and grace
Saving the human race.

Is this the end of the Story?
I would gladly take the nails
Rather than this piercing sword
Lodged in my heart.
You are my Son --
Not a king ---
Not a traitor ---
Not a messiah –
But my Son....
My Son....
My Son.

John 19: 1-5

*Then Pilate took Jesus and had him flogged. **2** The soldiers twisted together a crown of thorns and put it on his head. They clothed him in a purple robe **3** and went up to him again and again, saying, "Hail, king of the Jews!" And they slapped him in the face. **4** Once more Pilate came out and said to the Jews gathered there, "Look, I am bringing him out to you to let you know that I find no basis for a charge against him." **5** When Jesus came out wearing the crown of thorns and the purple robe, Pilate said to them, "Here is the man!"*

I Am the One

I am the one who held the whip
Stripping the flesh from Your back.
I pushed the crown of thorns
Until it pierced Your soul.

I pounded the nails
Holding You to the cross of splintered wood.
I lifted You up to the sky
A holy offering in an unholy place.

I pounded the cross into the ground
And You into its splintering wood
While You screamed in agony
I won Your robe
As You hung naked in the burning sun
I pierced Your side with my sword
Just to ensure Your death.
I did this.

I did this
As I quickly pass by
The desolate soul living on the street,
Pretending not to see.

I did this
As I remained silent
When a child was torn from her mother's side
Sacrificed for the taste of freedom
And the dream of a better life.

I did this
As the old woman weeps silent tears
Alone
While I gaze at my to do list
And do not see her name.

I did this.
I am the one.

Genesis 3: 22 - 24
22 And the Lord God said, "The man has now become like one of us, knowing good and evil. He must not be allowed to reach out his hand and take also from the tree of life and eat and live forever." 23 So the Lord God banished him from the Garden of Eden to work the ground from which he had been taken. 24 After he drove the man out, he placed on the east side of the Garden of Eden cherubim and a flaming sword flashing back and forth to guard the way to the tree of life.

John 10:10b
I have come that they may have life and have it to the full.

The Tree of Life

Battle engaged
Thunder rumbling
All heaven rages
Against the darkness
Even as their King hangs
Bleeding
Dying
On the eternal tree of life.

Holy Saturday

Matthew 16:24-25

24 Then Jesus told his disciples, "If anyone would come after me, let him deny himself and take up his cross and follow me. 25 For whoever would save his life will lose it, but whoever loses his life for my sake will find it.

The Battle Continues

The battle continues.
The Christ storms the gates of hell
Conquering this kingdom of evil
Wielding the sword of God
Releasing all prisoners
Guiding them out of the darkness
Into light.

Victory is ours
Even as the world holds its breath
Waiting outside the tomb.

John 1: 1-5

In the beginning was the Word, and the Word was with God, and the Word was God. 2 He was with God in the beginning. 3 Through him all things were made; without him nothing was made that has been made. 4 In him was life, and that life was the light of all mankind. 5 The light shines in the darkness, and the darkness has not overcome it.

He Descended into Hell

He descended into hell
Gathering around him
Forsaken souls
Thinking they were God abandoned.
Setting them free
He guided them
Stumbling and doubting
Out of darkness into the light.

Easter Sunday

Genesis 2: 7
Then the LORD God formed a man from the dust of the ground and breathed into his nostrils the breath of life, and the man became a living being.

Luke 24: 2-6a
2 They found the stone rolled away from the tomb, 3 but when they entered, they did not find the body of the Lord Jesus. 4 While they were wondering about this, suddenly two men in clothes that gleamed like lightning stood beside them. 5 In their fright the women bowed down with their faces to the ground, but the men said to them, "Why do you look for the living among the dead? 6 He is not here; he has risen!"

Easter Born

A Father's loving touch
The Word made flesh

And so God breathed
The very breath of God into him
And said Let there be Life!
And there was life.

Cold stone tumbled away
Releasing the tomb.

Cold flesh stirred in triumphant victory.

So is Easter born.

Matthew 28:2-6a

2 There was a violent earthquake, for an angel of the Lord came down from heaven and, going to the tomb, rolled back the stone and sat on it. 3 His appearance was like lightning, and his clothes were white as snow. 4 The guards were so afraid of him that they shook and became like dead men. 5 The angel said to the women, "Do not be afraid, for I know that you are looking for Jesus, who was crucified. 6 He is not here; he has risen, just as he said. Come and see the place where he lay."

Easter's Symphony

Let the trumpets call out Alleluia
With angels' triumph songs
Have the flutes trill with the birds
While rocks rumble with tympanic thunder
Releasing the music of the spheres
Honoring creation's rebirth.

Eastertide.

Mark 16: 6-8

6 "Don't be alarmed," he said. "You are looking for Jesus the Nazarene, who was crucified. He has risen! He is not here. See the place where they laid him. 7 But go, tell his disciples and Peter, 'He is going ahead of you into Galilee. There you will see him, just as he told you.'" 8 Trembling and bewildered, the women went out and fled from the tomb. They said nothing to anyone, because they were afraid.

What If....

What if the first ending were the only truth?
Then or now
They told no one.
Hugging the impossible
In dark chambers of their hearts.

What if they kept it hidden?
How then would we celebrate
A saving death
A new born life?

Would all the world keep silent
Instead of trumpets blaring
On the occasion of this celebration?

Mark 16: 1-4

When the Sabbath was over, Mary Magdalene, Mary the mother of James, and Salome bought spices so that they might go to anoint Jesus' body. 2 Very early on the first day of the week, just after sunrise, they were on their way to the tomb 3 and they asked each other, "Who will roll the stone away from the entrance of the tomb?" 4 But when they looked up, they saw that the stone, which was very large, had been rolled away.

Sing Us into Light

The stone is heaved away
Its power broken
Releasing the imprisoned
Melodies of life
Singing us into the light
Of the world's new day

John 20: 15 - 16
*Jesus asked Mary, "Woman, why are you crying? Who is it you are looking for?" Thinking he was the gardener, she said, "Sir, if you have carried him away, tell me where you have put him, and I will get him." **16** Jesus said to her, "Mary." She turned toward him and cried out in Aramaic, "Rabboni!" (which means "Teacher").*

Everything Became Clear

I did not recognize Him.
How often must I — must we —
Confess this?
How often is it true?
I did not recognize Him
Until He said my name.
Then
Suddenly
In that very moment I knew.
The past
The present
The future
Eternity
Became suddenly clear
And I rejoiced.

Luke 24: 13-16; 28-29

13 Now that same day two of them were going to a village called Emmaus, about seven miles from Jerusalem. 14 They were talking with each other about everything that had happened. 15 As they talked and discussed these things with each other, Jesus himself came up and walked along with them 16 but they were kept from recognizing him... 28 As they approached the village to which they were going, Jesus continued on as if he were going farther. 29 But they urged him strongly, "Stay with us, for it is nearly evening; the day is almost over." So he went in to stay with them. 30 When he was at the table with them, he took bread, gave thanks, broke it and began to give it to them. 31 Then their eyes were opened, and they recognized him.

The Road Home

Walking along the dusty road
Leaving Jerusalem
Headed for home
In Emmaus
We found the place of
Our true belonging
Our true joy
In His words.
God's Son revealed.

John 20: 24-29

24 Now Thomas (also known as Didymus), one of the Twelve, was not with the disciples when Jesus came. 25 So the other disciples told him, "We have seen the Lord! "But he said to them, "Unless I see the nail marks in his hands and put my finger where the nails were, and put my hand into his side, I will not believe." 26 A week later his disciples were in the house again, and Thomas was with them. Though the doors were locked, Jesus came and stood among them and said, "Peace be with you!" 27 Then he said to Thomas, "Put your finger here; see my hands. Reach out your hand and put it into my side. Stop doubting and believe." 28 Thomas said to him, "My Lord and my God!" 29 Then Jesus told him, "Because you have seen me, you have believed; blessed are those who have not seen and yet have believed."

Thomas

Away from the others
Alone in his despair
Thomas remembered
With grief's own longing

Long walks and longer talks
Along unknown paths
Being shown the Way

Grace.
Love.
Peace.
Sacrifice.
Words of challenge
Leading to commitment.

Drawn back to the place of feasting
A night, a day, a lifetime ago
The lamb of freedom
The bread of life
The wine of grace
Bits and pieces
Scattered about the sacred table.

His doubts
Reflect our own.

We ask together
How could it be
That the Lord of heaven
Would die and rise
For such a one as me?

The question lingers through eternity
Then suddenly Truth appears.

He is risen!
He is risen indeed!

www.ingramcontent.com/pod-product-compliance
Lightning Source LLC
Chambersburg PA
CBHW052203110526
44591CB00012B/2060